JEFFERSON COUNTY LIBRARY

Donated by

Northwest Friends of the Library

THE 12 MOST INFLUENTIAL
MUSICIANS OF ALL TIME

by Jeanne Marie Ford

12 STORY LIBRARY

www.12StoryLibrary.com

12-Story Library is an imprint of Bookstaves and Press Room Editions

Produced for 12-Story Library by Red Line Editorial

Photographs ©: Matt Sayles/Invision/AP Images, cover, 1; GeorgiosArt/iStockphoto, 4; FierceAbin/iStockphoto, 5; William Gottlieb/William P. Gottlieb Collection/Library of Congress, 6, 28; prophoto14/Shutterstock Images, 7; RCA Victor/AP Images, 8; Malgorzata Litkowska/Shutterstock Images, 9; Bettmann/Getty Images, 10; s_bukley/Shutterstock Images, 11; Dan Grossi/AP Images, 12; Don Ryan/AP Images, 13; J. Maum/AP Images, 14; Chris Pizzello/Invision/AP Images, 15, 29; Langevin/Str/AP Images, 16; MarkFGD/iStockphoto, 17; Doug Pizac/AP Images, 18; Music4mix/Shutterstock Images, 19; andreynikolaev.com/Shutterstock Images, 20; JStone/Shutterstock Images, 21; George Gongora/Corpus Christi Caller-Times/AP Images, 22; Merrick Morton/New Line Cinema/AP Images, 23; Debby Wong/Shutterstock Images, 24; Featureflash Photo Agency/Shutterstock Images, 25; Evan Agostini/Invision/AP Images, 27

Library of Congress Cataloging-in-Publication Data
Names: Ford, Jeanne Marie, 1971- author.
Title: The 12 most influential musicians of all time / by Jeanne Marie Ford.
Description: Mankato, MN : 12 Story Library, [2017] | Series: The most influential | Includes bibliographical references and index.
Identifiers: LCCN 2016047128 (print) | LCCN 2016048181 (ebook) | ISBN 9781632354112 (hardcover : alk. paper) | ISBN 9781632354822 (pbk. : alk. paper) | ISBN 9781621435341 (hosted e-book)
Subjects: LCSH: Musicians--Biography--Juvenile literature.
Classification: LCC ML3929 .F66 2017 (print) | LCC ML3929 (ebook) | DDC 780.92/2--dc23
LC record available at https://lccn.loc.gov/2016047128

Printed in the United States of America
022017

Access free, up-to-date content on this topic plus a full digital version of this book. Scan the QR code on page 31 or use your school's login at 12StoryLibrary.com.

Table of Contents

Mozart's Music Lives On

Wolfgang Amadeus Mozart is one of the most influential musicians of all time. He was born in Austria in 1756. At age three, Mozart learned to play the harpsichord. Two years later, he wrote his first piece of music.

Mozart's father knew his son was talented. He took Mozart on tour when he was six years old. He played music at royal courts, churches, and concert halls. Young Mozart became famous across Europe. He continued his travels and heard different styles of music along the way. They influenced his own style.

During his career, Mozart composed different styles of music. One of his most famous pieces is called "Eine Kleine Nachtmusik." Mozart wrote this lively music for violins, violas, cellos, and basses in 1787. Most people are still familiar with its melody today.

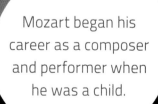

Mozart began his career as a composer and performer when he was a child.

CLASSICAL MUSIC

Classical musicians wrote in many styles. Sonatas were written for a single instrument or a small group of instruments. They are often short. Symphonies are long pieces of music written for a full orchestra. A concerto blends both styles. One instrument is featured among a larger group.

626
Number of Mozart's known compositions.

- Born in 1756, Mozart became one of the greatest composers of all time.
- He was an accomplished musician as a young child.
- He was inspired by and inspired many other musicians.

Mozart died in 1791. More than 250 years later, people still love his music. Musicians play it at concerts and church services. Students learn it in music lessons. Even television commercials and pop music borrow from Mozart's work.

During Mozart's era, the harpsichord was a common instrument.

Billie Holiday Sings the Blues

Billie Holiday is one of America's most famous jazz singers. She was born in 1915 and grew up in Baltimore, Maryland. Holiday's childhood was hard. She grew up in a poor family. She quit school in fifth grade.

At age 12, Holiday and her mother moved to Harlem, New York. There, Holiday began to sing in clubs. Holiday used her soulful voice to sing jazz songs in a new way. Usually jazz songs were upbeat. Holiday sang the songs slowly, using a quiet, husky voice. She was also one of the earliest female jazz singers to improvise.

Holiday did not have any voice training and could not read music. That did not matter, though. Thirty-eight of her songs made it onto the music

Born as Eleanora Fagan, she adopted the stage name Billie Holiday when she began singing.

charts. She performed on Broadway and with several jazz orchestras. It wasn't always easy. Holiday faced discrimination because she was black.

Holiday died in 1959. Her influence still has a far reach. In 1999, her hit "Strange Fruit" was named Song of the Century. Her life story was made into a movie and Broadway show. She still inspires current musicians, such as Norah Jones and Erykah Badu. Many people consider Holiday one of the best female jazz singers of all time.

The newly invented microphone allowed Holiday's hushed tones to be heard even in the furthest seats of a club.

350

Number of songs Holiday is known to have performed in her lifetime.

- Holiday sang many hit songs but faced discrimination.
- Holiday improvised when she sang.
- Today, many people consider Holiday the all-time best female jazz singer.

JAZZ MUSIC

In the early 1900s, a new form of music called jazz began in New Orleans, Louisiana. Jazz began in black communities. It is a mix of classical music and traditional slave songs. The piano, banjo, bass, and clarinet are common instruments in jazz bands. Often jazz singers improvise. They make up sounds and words for songs as they go, rather than planning them out.

Elvis Is the King of Rock and Roll

One of rock's first stars was Elvis Presley. He was born in 1935 to a poor family in Mississippi. At age 10, he won second prize in a singing contest. His mother saw his interest in music. She gave him a guitar as his next birthday gift. In 1953, Presley recorded his first song.

Gospel, country, and blues music inspired Presley. He used those styles in a new, modern way. Presley was also young and handsome. His good looks and fresh sound appealed to young fans. He quickly grew popular and appeared on radio, film, and television.

Many Americans viewed Presley as a rebel. Since he was white, some saw his use of gospel and blues, which were traditionally black styles of music, as controversial. Both black and white Americans disapproved of this for different reasons. Presley also had daring dance moves, where he swung his hips wildly. This, too, met with disapproval. Despite his

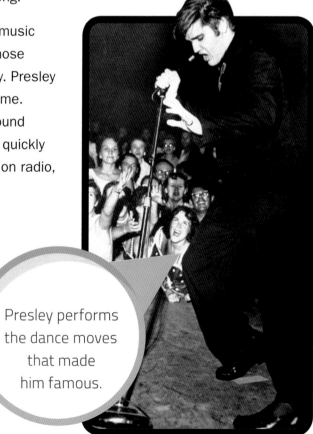

Presley performs the dance moves that made him famous.

Each year, more than 500,000 fans visit Graceland, Presley's home in Memphis, Tennessee.

critics, Presley's popularity grew. Fans called him the "King of Rock and Roll."

Presley died in 1977. Even after his death, Elvis remains a legend. He is one of the best-selling musicians of all time. His fans have bought 1 billion copies of his music. More than 100 of his songs have been in the top 40 charts. Presley made rock and roll music part of daily life in the United States. It formed the foundation of modern rock music.

MUSIC CHARTS

Music charts list the most popular songs and albums in a period of time. Each week, *Billboard* publishes the charts. Its experts count how many albums a musician sells. They also look at how often a musician's songs are streamed or downloaded. Musicians with the highest numbers are at the top of the charts.

18
Number of Elvis Presley's number one hits.

- He was called the "King of Rock and Roll."
- Blues, gospel, and country singers inspired Presley's early music.
- Presley starred in 33 films.

The Supremes Reign Supreme

In 1959, producer Berry Gordy founded Motown Records in Detroit. He was looking for musicians with a new sound. In 1961, Gordy signed an all-female group to Motown Records. Its members were Diana Ross, Florence Ballard, and Mary Wilson. They became known as the Supremes.

The Supremes combined pop and soul music. When they performed, they often dressed alike in fancy gowns. They had style, glamour, and a fresh sound. Their music found many fans. They were one of the first groups that appealed to white and black audiences alike.

The Supremes had a smooth, harmonious sound.

5

Number of number one hits the Supremes had in a row in 1965.

- The Supremes were one of Motown's most famous acts.
- They were known for their glamorous image.
- They were among the first black groups to appeal widely to white audiences.

After leaving the Supremes in 1970, Diana Ross had a successful solo career.

The Supremes had 12 number one songs. They sold out concert halls and sang on television. Their wide appeal gave them new opportunities. They were allowed to sing in places that did not usually welcome black artists.

Ballard and Ross had left the Supremes by 1970. As new members joined and left, the group's popularity went down. But their influence remains large. In 1988, they entered the Rock & Roll Hall of Fame. *Dreamgirls* was a Broadway musical and a movie that tells the story of the group's success.

The Beatles Lead the British Invasion

The Beatles were one of the very first boy bands. Their sound was different from anything that had come before. It was a mix of rock and roll, folk, and pop music. Over time, the group experimented with new sounds. They grew from a teen band into musicians who influenced the world. In 1956, John Lennon formed a band in Liverpool, England.

It became known as the Beatles in 1960. The band had four members. Lennon and Paul McCartney sang and played guitar. Ringo Starr played the drums. George Harrison played lead guitar.

The Beatles had their first number one hit in Great Britain in 1963. In early 1964, the Beatles came to the United States to sing on *The Ed Sullivan Show*. They performed

Beatlemania swept the United States after the band performed on *The Ed Sullivan Show*.

Albums made by Apple Records featured the company's logo, a green apple.

"I Want to Hold Your Hand." It was an instant hit. In April, the top five songs in the United States were all sung by the Beatles.

The Beatles craze that swept the nation was called Beatlemania. In 1968, the Beatles formed their own music label, Apple Records. It changed the focus of record-making from singles to entire albums. The Beatles also made films, which paved the way for music videos.

The Beatles broke up in 1970. Their music is still popular today. They are the best-selling band of all time. In December 2015, the Beatles' songs became available to stream. In the first six months, fans streamed the music more than 1 billion times.

73 million
Number of viewers who saw the Beatles' first appearance on *The Ed Sullivan Show*.

- The wide popularity of the group became known as Beatlemania.
- The Beatles are the world's best-selling band of all time.
- The films made by the Beatles inspired early music videos.

The Rolling Stones Rock On

British musicians Mick Jagger and Keith Richards joined with friends to form a band in 1962. The group called themselves the Rolling Stones. In 1962, the Rolling Stones gave their first concert at a club in London, England. The band's sound was part blues and part rock and roll. It was raw and edgy compared to the light, upbeat pop music of the time.

Many of the band's early songs were covers. They played songs by legendary blues musicians, such as Chuck Barry and Fats Domino. Before long, Jagger and Richards wanted to write their own music for the band. Their first big hit as songwriters was "(I Can't Get No) Satisfaction." In June 1965, it became the band's first number one song in the United States.

The band made several more hit rock songs in the late 1960s. As music styles changed in the 1970s and 1980s, so did the band's music.

Lead singer Mick Jagger struts across the stage at a concert in 1971.

They experimented with disco, punk, country, and other music styles. The band toured the world, putting on concerts for their fans. Jagger's energy, dance moves, and strut across the stage became legendary.

The Rolling Stones have spanned more than 50 years as rock stars. During that time, they have recorded 29 studio albums, released 109 singles, and put on thousands of

Mick Jagger's stage presence has become one of the band's trademarks.

concerts. Today, the band still draws record crowds to their concerts. Their sound has defined rock and roll for 50 years. Their sound and image have inspired many of today's heavy metal and hard rock bands.

250 million
Estimated number of albums the Rolling Stones have sold.

- The Rolling Stones were part of the British Invasion.
- Mick Jagger and Keith Richards have performed together for more than 50 years.
- The band's sound and image influenced many hard rock and heavy metal performers.

THE ROCK & ROLL HALL OF FAME

In 1995, the Rock & Roll Hall of Fame opened in Cleveland, Ohio. The site honors rock's most talented musicians. It features interviews, concert footage, and items that tell the story of rock and roll. Its members are considered the greatest rock musicians of all time.

Bob Marley Leads a Revolution

Robert Marley was born on the island of Jamaica in 1945. The island's music inspired him, especially reggae. It is a style of music that began in Jamaica. It has a strong, slow beat. Reggae features drums, guitars, and scrapers. In 1962, Marley formed a reggae band called the Wailers. The band began to mix pop and rock sounds with reggae. No one had done this before.

Marley's music also had a strong message to it. Marley had become a Rastafarian when he was younger. Rastafari is a set of religious and political beliefs that began in Jamaica. It is based on the Bible and traditional African beliefs. It calls for equal treatment no matter a person's skin color. Marley's music reflected these ideas.

In Jamaica, Marley was sometimes attacked for his beliefs. In 1976, he was shot while

Marley used his music to share his beliefs about peace and equality.

30,000
Number of people who attended Bob Marley's memorial service.

- His songs called for social justice and racial equality.
- Bob Marley was part of the Rastafarian movement.
- He brought reggae music to the world.

THE SOUNDS OF A SCRAPER

One of the instruments commonly used in reggae is called a scraper. It is a grooved piece of wood. A musician rubs a smooth stick across the scraper to the beat of the music. The result is a rasping sound with a strong rhythm.

rehearsing for a concert. That did not stop Marley. He still performed the show two days later. Marley continued to make music until 1981, when he died of cancer.

At the time of his death, Marley had sold more than 20 million albums. He introduced reggae music to the world. His messages of justice and equality still move fans today. His family now runs The Bob Marley Foundation. It helps poor people around the world.

The scraper helps to give reggae its unique sounds.

Michael Jackson Moonwalks to Stardom

Pop star Michael Jackson started singing at an early age. When he was five, he became the lead singer of a family band. It was called the Jackson 5. At age 13, Jackson started a solo career. He began to write and produce his own songs.

Jackson's success peaked with the *Thriller* album in 1982. It sold more copies than any other album in history. *Thriller* had 10 number one songs and won 8 Grammy Awards. When *Thriller* was released, music videos were new. They were mostly made to sell an artist's song. Jackson changed that with *Thriller*. He turned music videos into an art.

Jackson's video for the song "Thriller" was 14 minutes long, and it told a story that went with the song. It blended theater, dance, and music in a way television viewers had never seen. Jackson had set the standard for all future music videos.

In 1987, Jackson released his next album, *Bad*. The pop album was successful, producing five

Jackson's stage presence, dance moves, and unique sound made him a superstar.

number one songs. It was not as successful as *Thriller*, though. Critics gave the album bad reviews. Jackson continued to make music after *Bad*, but he never regained his earlier popularity. Jackson died in 2009.

During his career, Jackson earned the nickname the "King of Pop." He transformed music videos from sales pieces to works of art. His writing, singing, and dancing continue to influence musicians today.

37
Number of weeks *Thriller* was the number one album in the United States.

- Michael Jackson began performing as a child.
- *Thriller* is the best-selling album in history.
- Jackson was called the "King of Pop" for his talents as a singer, songwriter, dancer, and producer.

MICHAEL JACKSON
AUGUST 29, 1958 – JUNE 25, 2009

Fans in Los Angeles, California, sign a memorial for Michael Jackson shortly after his death.

Madonna Pushes Boundaries

In 1958, Madonna Ciccone was born in Michigan. As a child, she dreamed of being either a nun or a movie star. Madonna's plans changed in 1980. That year, she joined her boyfriend's band as a drummer. Soon, she was the lead singer. In 1983, Madonna released her first solo pop album, *Madonna*.

Warner Brothers produced *Madonna*. Its leaders tried to control Madonna's image. They wanted to pick her clothes, songs, and dance moves. Madonna rebelled against this. She wore wild clothes and made shocking comments. She also sang about difficult topics, such as race and religion. Fans loved it. *Madonna* sold more than 5 million copies.

Madonna's skill at changing her look and sound have made her successful for more than three decades.

- Madonna was one of the biggest pop stars of the 1980s.
- She continues to have a successful career as a singer, actress, writer, and producer.
- She is the best-selling female singer of all time.

Madonna always puts on a show for fans.

Boosted by her success, Madonna continued making albums. On each one, she reinvented her image. One thing remained the same, though. Madonna always gained attention for pushing boundaries. Many people disliked this about Madonna. They wanted her music and videos banned. But her fans loved her, and she continued to make new music.

Madonna's career has spanned more than 30 years. In that time, she has become the best-selling female singer of all time. She has had more number one singles than any other artist in history. Before Madonna, most of rock's major stars had been men. She paved the way for strong, successful female pop stars.

THINK ABOUT IT

Many of the most successful musicians are also dancers, actors, producers, and more. They often perform in multiple ways. Is it necessary to have many different talents in order to be considered great?

10 Selena Soars with Tejano Music

Tejano is folk music that started among Mexican Americans living in Texas. Selena Quintanilla is known as the "Queen of Tejano." She was born in Texas in 1971. At age 10, she became the lead singer of her family's band, *Selena y los Dinos*.

She spoke only English, but her father taught her to sing in Spanish.

By age 16, Selena was a popular and award-winning Tejano singer. In 1990, she released the album *Ven Conmigo*. It was the first Tejano album to go gold. That means it sold more than 500,000 copies. In 1993, Selena won a Grammy Award for the best Mexican-American album.

Selena began work on her first English album. But she was murdered before she could finish it. She was only 23 years old when she died in 1995. The album, *Dreaming of You*, was released after Selena's death. It was a big success. The story of Selena's life was made into a movie in 1997, starring Jennifer Lopez.

Selena's success introduced Tejano music to a wider audience.

175,000

Number of copies of *Dreaming of You* sold on the day it was released.

- Selena began singing in her family's Tejano band at age 10.
- She died at age 23.
- The success of her English-language album after her death drew many fans to her Spanish-language music.

LATIN AMERICAN MUSIC

Latin American music has many styles. Its earliest influences were from Spain, Portugal, and Africa. The music that resulted has a wide variety of sounds. Tango, salsa, mariachi, samba, and merengue are just a few examples. These styles influence the sounds of many US singers today.

Selena's influence drew attention to the Latino community. Three weeks after Selena's death, *People* magazine published a Spanish edition devoted to the singer. It sold out quickly. It inspired *People* magazine to create a weekly Spanish edition. Many other businesses began marketing to the Latino community. Twenty years after Selena's death, she remains a role model for many in the Latino community and beyond.

Selena appeared in one movie before her life was cut short.

Jay Z Overcomes His Hard-Knock Life

Hip-hop music began in New York in the 1970s. It has roots in the blues. Hip-hop music often features deejays and rapping. Break dancing and graffiti art are also closely connected to hip-hop. Its artists often write songs based on their own lives.

Jay Z shortened his childhood nickname, "Jazzy," to "Jay Z" when he began his hip-hop career.

One of hip-hop's biggest stars is Jay Z. He was born as Shawn Corey Carter in 1969 in New York. He grew up in a poor home with a single mother. Carter began to rap as an escape from the violence in his neighborhood. Carter's rough

$1.5 million

Amount of money Jay Z raised in his first charity concert in 2015.

- Jay Z is one of the most successful rap and hip-hop artists of all time.
- He has been influential in business, politics, and charity work.
- In 2008, he married fellow singer Beyoncé.

childhood inspired a number of his songs.

In 1989, Carter recorded a song with rapper Jaz-O. It was a success, and they appeared on MTV. Around this time, Carter changed his name to Jay Z. In 1996, he made his first album, *Reasonable Doubt*. It's now a hip-hop classic. In 1998, his song

THINK ABOUT IT

Jay Z and many other musicians often draw on personal experiences when writing songs. What reasons might inspire a musician to do this? Does a musician need to have a difficult life to write songs people will relate to?

"Hard-Knock Life" included music sampled from the musical *Annie*. It was a huge hit.

Soon Jay Z was the most popular hip-hop artist in the country. He also became a successful music producer. He started a clothing line and also got involved in politics and charity work. In 2008, he married singer Beyoncé. *Time* magazine named Jay Z one of the "Most Influential People of 2013."

Jay Z and his wife, Beyoncé, are a musical power couple. They have each sold approximately 28 million albums.

25

Taylor Swift Rises Swiftly to Fame

In 1989, Taylor Alison Swift was born in Pennsylvania. By the time Swift was five years old, she was writing her own songs. At age 10, she was singing professionally. Swift dreamed of becoming a country singer. When Swift was 14, she and her family moved to Nashville, Tennessee. It is where most country music is recorded.

Two years later, Swift released her first album, *Taylor Swift*. The album blended pop and country music. Her single "Tim McGraw" became a top 10 hit on the country charts. By 2008, she was the best-selling country artist in the United States. In 2010, she became the youngest person to win a Grammy for Album of the Year.

Over time, the singer has turned from country to pop music. In 2014, she released her first pop album,

1989. In its first week, it sold 1.3 million copies. It went on to win a Grammy for Album of the Year in 2015.

Swift's influence in the music world is strong. Her early songs made country music appeal to a wider audience. She has also used her fame to fight for fair pay for artists. She donates money for music education to children who might follow in her footsteps someday.

22
Number of Top 40 singles Taylor Swift produced between 2006 and 2010.

- Taylor Swift released her first hit album at age 16.
- She has had multiple hits as both a country and pop artist.
- She is the youngest Album of the Year Grammy winner.

THINK ABOUT IT

Many great musicians never had formal training. How much of their success is due to natural talent? Is music education important? Why?

In addition to singing, Swift is a skilled songwriter.

Other Notable Musicians

Guido d'Arezzo

Guido d'Arezzo lived in Italy in the eleventh century. He invented musical notation. It has been used by musicians from classical composers to today's pop stars.

Louis Armstrong

Louis Armstrong was one of the first famous jazz musicians. He played the trumpet, sang, acted, and led bands. He helped bring jazz to a wider audience.

Bob Dylan

Bob Dylan is an American singer and songwriter. His songs are known for their honesty and creativity. They have been covered and imitated by many. In 2016, Dylan won the Nobel Prize for Literature. It honored his work as a songwriter.

Ravi Shankar

Beginning in the 1960s, Ravi Shankar made music from India popular in the United States and Europe. He played the sitar, which is a stringed instrument.

Lang Lang

Chinese piano player Lang Lang was a gifted musician at a young age. He is now an international superstar. Millions of children have been inspired to take piano lessons after hearing him in concert.

Glossary

album
A group of songs released on the same record or CD.

cover
To sing a song that has already been recorded by someone else.

discrimination
Treating a person differently than others because of skin color, age, gender, or beliefs.

harpsichord
An instrument with a keyboard, similar to a piano.

improvise
To create something in the moment, rather than planning it out.

orchestra
A large group of musicians that includes many who play stringed instruments, such as the violin or viola.

produce
To create a product that can be sold, such as a music album.

rebel
One who fights against a person or group that holds power.

single
A song that is released on its own. It can also usually be found on an album.

For More Information

Books

Aretha, David. *Awesome African-American Rock and Soul Musicians*. Berkeley Heights, NJ: Enslow Publishers, 2013.

Robertson, Robbie. *Legends, Icons & Rebels: Music That Changed the World*. Toronto: Tundra Books, 2013.

Sandler, Martin W. *How the Beatles Changed the World*. New York: Walker Books for Young Readers, 2014.

Visit 12StoryLibrary.com

Scan the code or use your school's login at **12StoryLibrary.com** for recent updates about this topic and a full digital version of this book. Enjoy free access to:

- Digital ebook
- Breaking news updates
- Live content feeds
- Videos, interactive maps, and graphics
- Additional web resources

Note to educators: Visit 12StoryLibrary.com/register to sign up for free premium website access. Enjoy live content plus a full digital version of every 12-Story Library book you own for every student at your school.

Editor's note: The 12 topics featured in this book are selected by the author and approved by the book's editor. While not a definitive list, the selected topics are an attempt to balance the book's subject with the intended readership. To expand learning about this subject, please visit **12StoryLibrary.com** or use this book's QR code to access free additional content.

Index

About the Author

Jeanne Marie Ford is an Emmy-winning TV scriptwriter and holds an MFA in Writing for Children from Vermont College. She has written numerous children's books and articles and also teaches college English. She lives in Maryland with her husband and two children.